THIS CAN HELP SOMEONE

Cover photography by Jeff Smith

Interior photography by London Durham

THIS CAN HELP SOMEONE

REAL HELP FOR REAL PEOPLE

STIKKS

Dedicated to the love of my life. You are my best friend and the best husband any woman could ever ask for. Thank you for your endless support and encouragement. Just when I think I'm on to something "good", you come in pushing me into GREATNESS.

Table of Help

THIS CAN HELP SOMEONE

THIS CAN HELP SOMEONE

DAY ONE

Do Not Get Discouraged

The moment you say, "Yes God. Yes to your will. Yes to your ways," BOOM! —the enemy goes, *Oh no, you don't!*

Do you know that the enemy will leave you alone as long as you're not trying to walk in your purpose? If you're just working a job, paying bills, going to church, and not doing anything for the Kingdom of God, then the enemy isn't going to bother you. The enemy doesn't feel threatened because you aren't a threat! The moment you realize you've been living only for yourself and you're ready to give your life over to God, the enemy then comes in for the attack. He comes in to discourage you, rob you of your peace, and do everything he can to steal your faith from you. The last thing the enemy wants is for you to trust God.

The moment you begin to seek God's will for your life, and walk in your purpose, the enemy will get off his beach chair to come see what you're up to. You can't start living for God and think that life is going to be smooth sailing for you. The enemy doesn't want to see you saved, or anyone you could possibly have influence over get saved; so he will come in and try to turn your world completely upside down. The enemy will work hard to try and get you to forfeit God's blessings and plans for your life. DON'T LET HIM!

Please, understand that God doesn't have something ordinary for you. Oh no, no, no! God has a plan for your life, which is greater than anything you could've ever thought up on your own, and the enemy knows that. The enemy is no stranger to God's power. When you

When you begin to allow God to use you, it's going to be powerful...

begin to allow God to use you, it's going to be powerful, and you will become a threat to the kingdom of darkness. The enemy would love for you to give up. The enemy would love for you to just throw in the towel because life is too hard, but you can't do that—you've gone too far to do that! DO NOT THROW IN THE TOWEL. Don't get discouraged when you are under attack. Don't get discouraged if you feel like everything that could possibly go wrong is already going wrong. Don't get discouraged! God is with you! God loves you! God will protect you! Did you hear that? GOD WILL PROTECT YOU!

When you encounter trials, temptations, and difficulties while seeking God, it is a clear indication that you are on the right track. This is good news! Keep going!

Joshua 1:9 (NIV)

9. Have I not commanded you? Be Strong and courageous. Do not be afraid; do not be discouraged, for the LORD your God will be with you wherever you go.

THIS CAN HELP SOMEONE

DAY TWO

Do you want to know how to stress yourself completely out? Try to please everyone. If you're constantly focused on what everyone else wants you to do, you will rob yourself of peace. You will be the one stressed out while those causing the stress are at home on the couch with their feet up drinking lemonade.

People-pleasing can leave you feeling exhausted, unappreciated, and emotionally drained. The funny part or not so funny part is, NO ONE IS EVER HAPPY! You spend all your time and energy trying to listen to everyone and please everyone, only to hear complaints, only to hear how you could've done a better job, and only to hear the grunts of a bunch of dissatisfied people! If you let the judgment or thoughts of people dictate your every move, you will eventually find yourself being everyone's puppet.

Look at it this way: If you go right, people will say, "Why didn't you go left?" If you go left, people will say, "Why didn't you go right?" Oh, and don't you dare stand still, because then people will say, "Why the heck didn't you move?!" So what do you do? The answer is, STOP TRYING TO PLEASE EVERYONE! It can't be done! You're on an impossible mission here, especially if you're trying to please a bunch of NEGATIVE people!

People who are negative won't take a break from being negative just for you. They will continue to be negative until they get their own healing and breakthrough. You shouldn't look to negative people for advice or direction. They will always end up making you feel bad

Don't look to negative people for advice…

about the decisions you make. Don't look to negative people for advice and don't share your good news with them. They will suck the life and joy out of you until you are as unhappy as they are.

The fact of the matter is, everyone will not always be on board with your decisions, and that's OK. Don't get wrapped up in what everyone wants you to be, what everyone wants you to say, or what everyone wants you to do, because there's really only one opinion that matters and that's God's. It's the only opinion that should dictate how you live your life.

What is God calling you to do? Is He calling you to go right or left? Maybe He's calling you to be still. This is the only *pleasing* you should be concerned about. It's the only pleasing that matters. It's the only pleasing with real rewards that last beyond this life.

God's approval is the only approval you need. Today, say *no* to people-pleasing, and *YES* to God-pleasing!

Galatians 1:10 (NLT)

10. Obviously, I'm not trying to win the approval of people, but of God. If pleasing people were my goal, I would not be Christ's servant.

THIS CAN HELP SOMEONE

DAY THREE

God Knows What You Need

Do you think God needs you to tell Him what you need? Do you think God is trying to figure out solutions to your problems as you pray? Do you think you can tell God something He doesn't already know? The answer to all of these questions is, *No!* God knows it all.

Prayer is not for God. Prayer is FOR YOU! Prayer reveals your need for God. Prayer shows that you have faith. Prayer gives you the opportunity to witness God's power because when you pray, THINGS CHANGE. Sometimes things change instantly and sometimes things change gradually, but it all began with a prayer.

Now, things may not look and change exactly the way YOU were expecting them to, but that's when you have to trust God and understand that His thoughts are far greater, better, and wiser than your thoughts. That's right; you're not smarter than God. The creation is not wiser than the Creator.

When you pray, you won't always get the answer you're looking for. It might not look like what you thought it should look like. It may even feel uncomfortable, but guess what? You can rest assured that God is listening to you. He hears even the silent prayer that you won't speak out, for He hears it in your heart. No prayer is insignificant to God.

No prayer is insignificant to God.

12

The enemy will try to make you believe that God doesn't care, and that God isn't listening, but those are LIES! Pray and watch God show up!

God is listening and God knows exactly what you need before you say a word. Even while your need is only a thought in your head, God has already made provision for you. He's just waiting for you to pray in faith and believe that He is able. DON'T DOUBT GOD! Believe with all you heart! Believe with all your soul! Believe today and watch Him provide.

Philippians 4:19 (KJV)

19. But my God shall supply all your needs according to his riches in glory by Christ Jesus.

THIS CAN HELP SOMEONE

DAY FOUR

How many times have you been worried and your problems were solved because you worried hard enough? Were your problems ever solved because you worried long enough? When is the last time you 'worried your problems away'?

Worrying never helps. Worrying never calms. Worrying is never healthy. If you think about it, WORRYING SUCKS! It sucks the life out of you. It sucks the joy out of you. It sucks the peace out of you—the very peace that God promised you would have IF you keep your mind on Him. You rob yourself of peace when you worry.

You can't fully trust God and worry at the same time.

You can't fully trust God and worry at the same time. It's a contradiction. They speak two different languages. Worry says, *"I'm hopeless."* Trust says, "I'm confident." Worry says, "Nothing will change." Trust says, "This too will pass." Worry says, "I will lose." Trust says, "I always win." Do you see the difference? Are you speaking a language of worry or trust?

Worrying is not wise. If you can't change a situation, why worry about it? NOTHING WILL CHANGE. If you can change a situation, why worry about it? JUST CHANGE IT.

What are you most worried about today? What is it? Is it about a job, money, health, kids, marriage, dating, school? What's worrying you the most? Will you make the decision to stop worrying today? Right here, right now, give all of your worries to God. Tell Him you no longer want them. Tell Him you no longer want to be in control. Let all of your worries go and allow God to be God in your life. Everything that is weighing you down right now, God is saying, "Give it to me." Will you do it? Will you hand over your worries to God? Today, trade in your worry for peace.

Matthew 6:25-27 (NLT)

25. That is why I tell you not to worry about everyday life—whether you have enough food and drink, or enough clothes to wear. Isn't life more than food, and your body more than clothing? 26. Look at the birds. They don't plant or harvest or store food in barns, for your heavenly Father feeds them. And aren't you far more valuable to him than they are? 27 Can all your worries add a single moment to your life?

THIS CAN HELP SOMEONE

DAY FIVE

Have you ever noticed how some people are just better at certain things? Maybe you're not the best athlete or musician, but you can fix anything! Maybe you're not the best public speaker, but can write like no other. Maybe, you're not a science or math buff, but you have an amazing eye for photography. Sure, there are things that your friends are better at than you, but there are also things that you naturally do better than anyone else. This is because you were created for greatness!

God created you with a specific greatness inside of you and your greatness will not be the same as your neighbor's greatness. Don't let yourself get caught up in comparing your greatness to those around you, on TV, or on the Internet.

Did you know that God created you for a very specific purpose? That's right! Your birth was not a surprise to God. On the day you were born, God was not in heaven, saying, "Oh look, there's another baby born today. What should I do with this one?" No! God knew exactly who you were before you were born, and He made you for greatness.

Think about it, this book that you're reading right now, was created. It wasn't randomly typed up one day and then someone went, "Hmm... I guess I'll turn these words into a book." That's not how this book was created, and that's not how God created you.

The book was first an idea, and with that idea, a creation was born. God had an idea, and with that idea, you were born.

...God had an idea, and that idea was YOU.

Wow, how beautiful is it to know that God had an idea, and that idea was YOU. Let that marinate in your heart for a second.

You have to understand that there is no way that you're an idea from God and not full of greatness. Greatness is all God knows! Walk in your greatness today!

Jeremiah 1:5 (NCV)

5. Before I made you in your mother's womb, I chose you. Before you were born, I set you apart for special work...

THIS CAN HELP SOMEONE

DAY SIX

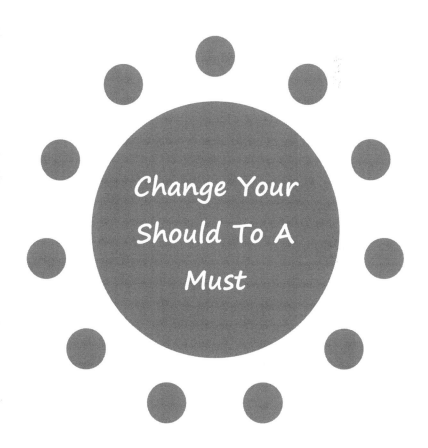

Change Your Should To A Must

Have you ever tried to quit a bad habit, finish an old project, or change something in your life for the better, and not succeed? People try to quit smoking, lose weight, get out debt, and the list goes on, only to come up short. It's a constant battle of starting and quitting, starting and quitting, starting and quitting.

What about those people who say they're going to do something and actually do exactly what they said they'd do? How does that happen? You have people giving up smoking cold turkey, losing 20 pounds in one month, decreasing their debt significantly until they are out of debt all together, and the list continues. Why is it that some people can stop bad habits while others can't? Why do some people start and never finish?

Unfortunately, to most people out there, changing will remain an idea never manifested, while there are others who think to change and actually DO. People who change have realized that change is a MUST.

Maybe you've found yourself wanting to change a particular area in your life. Maybe you have a dream in your heart that you've always wanted to pursue. Have you said to yourself, "I should..."? THERE LIES YOUR PROBLEM!

Stop giving yourself options and start saying, I must!

Anything that you "should" do is optional. Stop giving yourself options and start saying, *I must!* *I must lose weight, I must get out of debt, I must forgive, I must read more, I must pray, I MUST, I MUST, I MUST!*

When something is a MUST, you will DO it! What are some things you know you MUST change today? Don't wait for New Year's Eve to make a resolution. Change today! Right now! It doesn't matter how many times you've tried before and failed. That was your old "shoulds." Walk in your new MUST today!

Philippians 4:13 NCV

13. I can do all things through Christ, because he gives me strength.

THIS CAN HELP SOMEONE

DAY SEVEN

People Are Not Perfect

Stop expecting everyone and everything to be perfect. You can't expect everyone to make the right decisions all the time without any mistakes. That's ridiculous! You have to leave room for error. You have to leave room for mistakes. You have to leave room for apologies. Even those who love you THE MOST will get it wrong sometimes. Do you know why? Because people are flawed! No one here on this Earth is perfect! Not one! You're not even perfect!

Too many people are walking around upset. They are upset at their boss, co-workers, friends, pastor, spouse, kids, pets... STOP!

Where is your grace? You know grace, right? Grace is getting something good when you don't deserve it or NOT getting punished even though you actually DO deserve it. Grace is that thing you want from God even though you mess up EVERY SINGLE DAY. We all fall short in the eyes of God, but God still loves us. He still forgives you, AND He still blesses you!

When was the last time you did something nice for someone that didn't deserve it? It's easy to be nice to people who are nice to you. That's EASY! God is calling you to something bigger, something more meaningful. God wants

God wants you to show grace to the undeserving.

you to show grace to the undeserving. To that person who cut you off on the road, show GRACE! To that person who cut you in line at the grocery store, show GRACE! To that person who owes you money, show GRACE! To that person who hit your car, show GRACE! To the person that sat in your seat at church, show GRACE! There aren't assigned seats anyway! Grow up! It's all about GRACE! GRACE! GRACE! GRACE! Do you have it? If not, ask God to give it to you. Beg Him to fill you with grace to love those who mess up sometimes.

No more holding onto grudges for 15 years! You have to let go and surrender all of your hurts to God. Holding a grudge is physically and spiritually toxic. Let it go and release it to your Heavenly Father. You will not find a perfect church, friendship, relationship, or job. If you did find such things, it stopped being perfect the moment you showed up!

The reality of it all is people are not perfect. You are not perfect. No one is perfect, and that's OK! Today, take your perfect standards off people and give them grace instead. You'll feel a lot better about life and people.

Romans 3:23 (NLT)

23. *Everyone has sinned; we all fall short of God's glorious standard.*

THIS CAN HELP SOMEONE

DAY EIGHT

Have An Attitude Of Gratitude

No matter what is going on in your life right now, if you think hard enough, you can come up with something to be grateful for. If your car needs some repair, praise God you have a car! If your children are misbehaving, praise God you have children! If your job is stressful, praise God you have a job! If you're not getting along with you parents, praise God you have parents! If your spouse is getting on your nerves, praise God you're not alone!

There is always something to be grateful for, but you have to CHOOSE gratefulness. You can look at your life and choose to have a bad attitude or you can look at your life and choose to have gratitude.

Many times, the problems you have actually come from a blessing that you once prayed for. You prayed for a job, now you dread going to work. You prayed for a house, now you're upset every time something needs to be fixed. You prayed for a car, and now you constantly complain about gas prices. You prayed for a husband or wife, now you wish you were single.

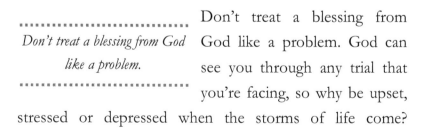

Don't treat a blessing from God like a problem.

Don't treat a blessing from God like a problem. God can see you through any trial that you're facing, so why be upset, stressed or depressed when the storms of life come?

Instead, get excited about what God is going to do in your life!

Hasn't God seen you through your problems in the past? If He helped you before, know that He'll help you now, and He will continue to help you in the future.

You have to get to a place in life where you can praise God through any circumstance. You can praise God when it's raining blessings and you can praise God when it's just raining.

God is always good! In every situation, God is still good! IT'S WHO HE IS. He doesn't stop being a Good God just because you've had a bad experience. The sooner you realize how good God is to you, the sooner you'll be able to have an attitude of gratitude.

1 Thessalonians 5:18 NLT

18. Be thankful in all circumstances, for this is God's will for you who belong to Christ Jesus.

THIS CAN HELP SOMEONE

DAY NINE

The enemy wants you to feel defeated, hopeless, and weak. There may be things going on in your life right now that are out of your control, but guess what? THEY ARE NOT OUT OF GOD'S CONTROL.

You don't serve a weak God! You're made in the image of an All-Powerful God! Think about it. If your parents are tall, you're tall. If your parents are athletic, you're athletic. If your parents are thin, you're thin. If your Heavenly Father is powerful, which He is, then YOU ARE POWERFUL!

Your prayers are powerful! When you pray, things change. You're not weak! You don't come from a weak

Your prayers are powerful!

family. You are a part of the greatest Kingdom of all time! You are a child of a King—not just a king, but *the* King of kings. There's no one before Him and there'll be no one after Him.

If you've been feeling weak lately, get with the plug. As long as you stay connected to the source of power, you will have strength. Keep God plugged into your life and watch His power manifest.

Don't let the enemy lie to you anymore. If you think you are defeated, THAT IS A LIE. If you think you are hopeless, THAT IS A LIE. If you think you can't make it another day, then like Maury says, THAT IS A LIE!

You have the Spirit of God in you! When you start to feel weak, remind yourself who your Father is! Remind yourself that you have power in you! God won't give you a situation that you can't handle. He knows you. He made you. Therefore, He knows EXACTLY how much you can handle.

Whatever you're dealing with in life right now, it's not too much. You are strong! You are powerful! You are tough enough to handle any and everything going on in your life right now, because you are connected to the ultimate source of strength.

Isaiah 40:29 (NCV)

29. He gives strength to those who are tired and more power to those who are weak.

THIS CAN HELP SOMEONE

DAY TEN

Love The Creator More Than The Creation

Stop reading this for 20 seconds and think about something or someone you really love. On a serious note, I mean, STOP READING please, just for 20 seconds until you figure out what it is…

Okay, do you have it? Do you have it in your head? Now, whatever you're thinking about, I want you to ask yourself this question, "Do I love _____ (fill in the blank) more than I love God?" Naturally, you may want to say *No*, but think about it some more. That thing or person that you love, do you think about it more than you think about God? Do you talk about it more than you talk about God? Do you know more things about it, than what you know about God? Are you known more for loving that particular thing or known more for loving God?

Often times, when people are asked if they love God, they quickly answer *yes*. When asked how they know that they love God, typically people start listing a bunch of things God has done for them over the years without ever mentioning anything that they've done for God. The only thing the list reveals is that God loves them. It doesn't communicate their love for God.

When you love something or someone, it is very evident. You show interest in things you love. There are actions behind loving something. Love

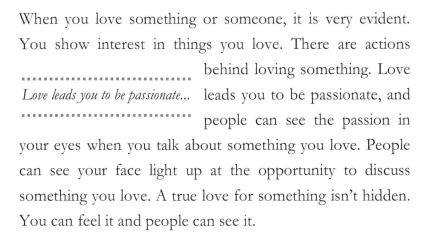

Love leads you to be passionate... leads you to be passionate, and people can see the passion in your eyes when you talk about something you love. People can see your face light up at the opportunity to discuss something you love. A true love for something isn't hidden. You can feel it and people can see it.

Can people see your love for God? Are you passionate when it comes to God and the things of God? Does growing in your faith even interest you? What actions are behind your love for God? Do you love God with actions or merely words?

If you want to love God with actions, but don't know how, have you asked God to reveal to you how you can love Him with your actions? Reading His Word is a great place to start. If someone you loved wrote you a letter, would you read it? God has written so much to you because He loves you. Read what He has to say and watch your passion for God grow. God desires your attention and wants you to be interested in Him.

There may be something you've been praying for, but God won't give it to you simply because you will pay more attention to the blessing instead of the One who has blessed you. God wants your affections set on Him and He's not going to give you things that will take your eyes, heart, and mind off Him. Your Heavenly Father deserves all of your love, all of your attention, and all of your admiration. Nothing or no one has done what God has done for you—nothing can take the credit for what God has given to you. You have to be careful that you're not worshipping and loving the things God created more than the Creator Himself.

Matthew 22:37 (NCV)

37. Jesus answered, "Love the Lord your God with all your heart, all your soul, and all your mind."

Stikks

Your Thoughts

THIS CAN HELP SOMEONE

DAY ELEVEN

Keep Moving Forward

Have you ever wondered if you were moving in the right direction? Maybe you made a career change, ended a relationship, moved away from home, changed your major in college, or made some other life-changing decision that left you wondering, *Was this what God wanted me to do?*

If you're not in the habit of asking God for direction, make it a habit today. There is nothing better than being in the will of God. Being in God's will simply means that you are doing what He planned for you to do. So are you? Are you doing what God planned for you to do? Are you living your life the way God planned for you to live it?

There is nothing better than being in the will of God.

Sometimes, when praying for God's will, you may not always hear His response. You may be praying about a career change, where to live, buying a new car, what church to attend, whom you should date…and the list goes on. So what do you do when you're unsure of what God is telling you to do?

When you don't hear a response from God or you don't hear a clear yes or no, that doesn't necessarily mean that you shouldn't do anything. Yes, there are times when you'll have to be patient and be still for a season. Sometimes, that is the best option for the situation, and it may be the only option that brings you peace when you're unsure of what to do. There's nothing wrong with that. But, there are also other instances where you may not know the answers, but you do know that God is calling you to trust Him, therefore you must KEEP MOVING FORWARD!

God always has a way of working everything out for you. He loves you so much and only wants what's best for you. Don't let the fear of the unknown stop you from moving forward in life. As long as your decision doesn't involve you deliberately disobeying God's Word, continue to move forward. When you are seeking God's will for your life, you can rest assured that He will reroute you if necessary.

Now, what you should be concerned about are God's "No's." Typically, you can CLEARLY hear and feel God's *No's*. A lot of His *No's* are clearly stated in His Word. There are some things you won't even have to pray about because you know that God is against it.

Then there are times when you feel God's *No*, but continue in your own decision anyway because you gave yourself a *yes*. THIS IS DANGEROUS. Don't give yourself a *yes* after God has already given you a *No*. Don't try to rationalize God's *NO* and turn it into a yes and don't go to your friends seeking a yes when you know God has already said *No*. No means no! God sees the bigger picture and if

He is giving you a *no*, it's for your benefit. No matter what you think you know, God knows more.

From now on, trust God's judgment over yours even when it doesn't make sense to you. God won't fail you.

Romans 8:28 (NAS)

28. And we know that God causes all things to work together for the good to those who love God, to those who are called according to His purpose.

Stikks

Your Thoughts

THIS CAN HELP SOMEONE

DAY TWELVE

It's very common to talk to your friends whenever you're having a problem. You talk to them about problems at work, with relationships, with family, money, health, your kids, school and the list of problems goes on and on. People love talking to friends about the issues and worries of life. It feels comforting, safe, and relieving. Here's the thing though: YOUR FRIENDS CAN'T FIX YOUR PROBLEMS!

What do friends typically do when you open up to them? They validate your feelings; take your side, and often times give bad advice. It's not intentional, but it happens. You can be completely wrong and at fault in a situation, but a friend will lead you to believe that you are totally justified and right. Friends tell you what you want to hear because they want to maintain the friendship. This is why it's very important to monitor whoever you discuss your problems with. Instead of just complaining to friends about life, seek counsel.

There's a big difference between seeking godly counsel and COMPLAINING. When you complain to your friends about your problems, they just join in on the complaining! You may hear things like, "You don't have to take that. Just quit," "If I got cheated on, I'd just cheat back," "I would've cussed him out too," or "You have to do what's best for you."

Venting your concerns to friends can be toxic at times. Instead of venting to friends, try talking to God. God is the one who can change your situation. In fact, your friends get tired of hearing about your

God is the one who can change your situation.

problems anyway. Think about that one friend you have, who is always calling to complain about things in his or her life. You dread picking up the phone because you know it's going to be about some drama. Don't be that friend! How many times do your friends really want to hear about your bad relationship or job?

There's good news, though. Do you know who is eager to listen to your problems 24 hours a day, 7 days a week? Your Heavenly Father! He wants to hear from you, and it never gets old! God, the Creator of heaven and earth, the Alpha and Omega, the King of kings and Lord of lords, desires an intimate relationship with you. He wants to hear and solve all of your problems. That's amazing!

Think of someone famous you would love to sit down and talk to. Think about it right now. Maybe it's a singer, athlete, or actor. Do you have the person in mind? Now, think about if that person wanted you to contact him or her. That would be crazy, right? You would hit the floor if you found out this particular famous person wanted to sit down and talk to you. Well, guess what? God is BIGGER than any celebrity you could think of and He wants to talk to you, listen to you, AND fix your problems! Stop treating God like a last resort, someone you turn to when no one else picks up the phone. Prayer shouldn't be your last option; it should be your first, because it's really the only sure way to a solution.

Psalms 66:19-20 (NCV)

19. But God has listened; he has heard my prayer. 20. Praise God, who did not ignore my prayer or hold back his love from me.

Stikks

Your Thoughts

THIS CAN HELP SOMEONE

DAY THIRTEEN

The sooner you realize what dating is for, the sooner you can stop getting upset, depressed, or stressed over someone leaving you. Breakups are part of dating. Just because you date someone for a few months or even a few years, doesn't automatically mean that's the person you will marry and spend the rest of your life with.

Though heartbreaking and sad, breakups are a component of dating that can't be avoided. If you can't handle a breakup, you may want to reevaluate whether or not you're ready to date. Breakups are inevitable and will happen. Even if you end up marrying your high school sweetheart, you'll still experience breakups along the way because dating for extended periods of time typically involves A LOT of "makeup breakup" cycles. Why? Because there's no real commitment involved.

Dating someone, or making someone your boyfriend or girlfriend, isn't the same as marriage. You may try to treat a dating relationship like marriage or paint a picture of marriage in your mind, but it simply isn't marriage. Dating and marriage ARE NOT EQUALS, so they shouldn't be treated as such.

Dating is used simply to see if you want to spend the rest of your life with that person, and if you don't, YOU GO! There's nothing wrong with that! YOU CAN LEAVE! That's the beauty of dating! Sometimes you will be the one to leave and sometimes you will be the one getting dumped. IT'S OK! Praise God that you won't be distracted by a meaningless dating relationship when your real spouse comes along! God wants to bless you, but He can't do it while you're holding onto someone else's husband or wife. THEY AREN'T YOURS. LET THEM "GET TO STEPPING"! God is clearing the way for your Mr. or Mrs. Right. And that doesn't mean you're going to get a perfect person. It just means the one that God sends will be perfect FOR YOU.

> *...the one that God sends will be perfect FOR YOU.*

You should never feel obligated to continue in a dating relationship that you don't foresee lasting forever. Why would you spend your valuable time in a relationship that you know isn't going to stand the test and trials of marriage? Leaving doesn't make you or the other person a "bad person" since the relationship isn't leading to wedding bells.

All relationships has its ups and downs. That's normal. But, there are situations where YOU KNOW the relationship isn't going to work out. Don't be afraid to break it off. Don't be afraid of getting dumped. Don't be afraid of starting over. You're doing both of you a favor in the long run. The worst thing you can do is hold on when God is telling you to let go.

Proverbs 3:5-6 (NLT)
5. Trust in the LORD with all your heart; do not depend on your own understanding. 6. Seek His will in all you do, and He will show you which path to take.

THIS CAN HELP SOMEONE

DAY FOURTEEN

Usually, when someone asks how you're doing, you respond by saying, "Good." It's a cliché response that really doesn't express how you're feeling at all, but it's popularly used to move you along in a conversation.

How different would a conversation go if you responded intentionally different from how people were expecting you to respond? How impactful could you be in a 10-second "hi and bye" conversation?

The next time someone asks you how you're doing, try responding by saying, "I'm Greeeeaaat!" Don't say, "Great or I'm Great" but say, "Greaaaat!" Say it just like that and see the response you get. Tell people how GREAT you're doing and watch them get intrigued by your greatness!

Sometimes, you might not feel too great towards life circumstances, but the reality is, YOU ARE GREAT! You're GREAT because you serve a GREAT God! A God that's GREATER than your worry, GREATER than your stress, GREATER than your finances, GREATER than your relationship problems, GREATER than your debt, GREATER than any sickness, GREATER than depression, GREATER than peer pressure, GREATER than unemployment, GREATER than your circumstances, Greater than....you fill in the blank! GOD IS GREEEAAT!

God is great; therefore, you are great! Whenever you find yourself having a bad day, remind yourself of how great God is. Remind yourself of how faithful God has been to you in the past. God's greatness doesn't run out. His greatness doesn't decrease when your worries increase. Great is who God is, now and forever more! You serve a great God who has already fought and won all of your battles! Go ahead and brag on God! The next time someone asks, *How are you?* tell them, *I'M GREAAAAT!*

God's greatness doesn't run out.

Psalms 147:5 (NIV)

5. *Great is our Lord and mighty in power; his understanding has no limit.*

THIS CAN HELP SOMEONE

DAY FIFTEEN

Your problems may come as a surprise to you, but they're not a surprise to God. God knows every difficult situation you will ever face here on earth. He knew what each day of your life would look like before you were even born. God is not working out your problems on a case-by-case basis. God isn't in heaven trying to figure out how to fix your situation. Your problems are already solved! Your situation is fixed!

You may not know how He's going to fix your problems or when He's going to fix them, but IT IS FINISHED. The only thing you have to do is praise Him because you know that whatever you're going through will come to an end. There's an expiration date on your problems. There is an ending to your suffering. There's an ending to your stress. There's an ending to your depression. Whatever your struggle, problem, or issue is, THERE IS AN ENDING. God has already solved every single problem you will ever have!

God has already solved every single problem you will ever have!

Don't let the worries of this life take your praise away. You may feel, at times, like God has forgotten you and your situation, but that is a lie from the enemy. Never allow yourself to believe that you aren't in God's thoughts. God is always thinking of you! The enemy wants you to feel deserted—alone and helpless, as if you don't have any help.

Never believe that. If you don't have anyone else around, know that you have your Heavenly Father right there with you.

You can have peace in the midst of a storm if you remember that you serve a God who is omniscient. That means, God is All-knowing. There is NOTHING that God doesn't know and more importantly, there is NOTHING that God doesn't know about YOU. God knows about the storm. He went before you and worked out your problems before you even encountered them!

Think back to a situation where you felt hopeless. You probably felt like God wasn't listening. You probably felt like God had turned His back on you. Maybe you stopped praising, stopped praying, stopped going to church, and stopped being full of joy. Then, in God's timing, what happened? HE WORKED IT OUT! He did it before and He will do it again and again...and AGAIN!

You don't have to worry about a single problem you have in your life. YOUR PROBLEMS ARE ALREADY SOLVED. It's time to walk in God's peace. He got you!

2 Chronicles 20:17 (NLT)

17. You will not even need to fight. Take your positions; then stand still and watch the Lord's victory. He is with you...

THIS CAN HELP SOMEONE

DAY SIXTEEN

Stop Closing Doors

People are so quick to talk about how a door closed on them, but what about the doors you close on yourself? You know the ones where you go: "I'm not smart enough," "I didn't go to school for that," "I'm not pretty enough," "I'm not thin enough," "I don't have any experience," "I don't have enough experience," "I'm too young," "I'm too old," or "They're more qualified than me."

Wait, Excuse me?!!!! God QUALIFIES the UNQUALIFIED! He's not looking at your age, experience, finances or any of that! What He's looking at is your FAITH. Have faith and believe that God can open any door for you and watch Him do it. God will work things out in your favor if you believe, have faith, and trust in His abilities over your own. God can give you favor in school, in your career, in relationships…. It's all about the FAVOR of God.

Did God put something in your heart for you to do that surpasses your natural ability? Does it feel overwhelming and maybe even impossible to accomplish? PERFECT! That's a perfect setup for God to come in and do the things that only He can do to accomplish His will and purpose for your life.

God wants to use you in a mighty way…

God wants to use you in a mighty way, but FIRST you have to take your hands off the door — no more closing doors and counting yourself out. You are never too young, too old, or too inexperienced to be used by God. You don't have to be the prettiest, smartest, or most talented. The only thing you have to be is WILLING.

Whatever God puts in your heart for you to accomplish, give Him a *yes* today. No matter how scary, big, or impossible it may seem, tell God *yes* and watch His favor get poured out on you!

Matthew 19:26 (NCV)

26. Jesus looked at them and said, "For people this is impossible, but for God all things are possible.

THIS CAN HELP SOMEONE

DAY SEVENTEEN

Everyone Steps
In Poop

Stepping in poop is a gross analogy, but it's so true! As long as you are here on this Earth, you WILL face adversity. There's no way around it. It doesn't matter if you're rich, poor, tall, short, married, or single, YOU WILL ENCOUNTER HARDSHIPS. You're going to step in it, roll around in it, and often times feel stuck in it.

Life is hard and sometimes, yes, it stinks, BUT there is an upside to this. When trials come into your life, you get to choose how you respond. During your hardships, you can respond in two ways.

One, you can find yourself stepping in the "poops of life" and respond by getting upset, frustrated, depressed, stressed, and overwhelmed. Or TWO, you can scoop it up and use it to grow.

Adversity is nothing more than fertilizer for your life. It will make you stronger, wiser, and more humble. Ultimately, you become more like who God wants you to be. Don't you want to be everything God created you to be? Don't you want to walk in everything God has laid out for your life?

If so, you're going to have to endure some sufferings that will help develop your character. Everything you go through is pushing you towards your purpose in life. You may not understand why you have to deal with all the problems you have, you may not understand why bad things happen to you, you may not understand why you seem to always get the short end of the stick, but you can rest assured that God doesn't waste pain.

God doesn't waste pain.

Every hurt, heartache, and trouble that you have ever felt has a definite purpose for your life. God is going to use it all for His glory. Trust His plans for your life and believe with all your heart that He has great and mighty things in store for you. No matter how crazy life can get, or how crazy your life may even look right now, God has a plan, and it is PERFECT.

Remember, trials are only temporary, but who you become in the process is life changing.

James 1:2-4 (NLT)

2 When troubles of any kind come your way, consider it an opportunity for great joy. 3 For you know that when your faith is tested, your endurance has a chance to grow. 4 So let it grow, for when your endurance is fully developed, you will be perfect and complete, needing nothing.

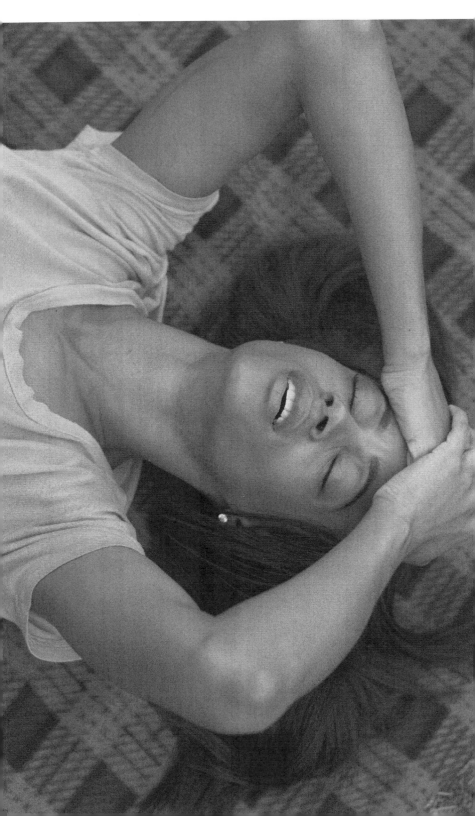

THIS CAN HELP SOMEONE

DAY EIGHTEEN

Stop Worrying About Messing Up

God's goodness is not contingent upon you being a good person. People have been messing up from the beginning and God has been good BEFORE the beginning. His goodness is everlasting and DOES NOT CHANGE. God is good because He's GOOD! It's who He is!

The enemy would love for you to focus on all of your shortcomings. The enemy would love for you to focus on all of your so-called failures, so that you're too distracted to focus on God's goodness.

When you focus on your failures, instead of God's goodness, what happens? You begin to feel defeated, hopeless, worthless, ashamed, and ultimately unloved by God. All of those thoughts and feelings are LIES. They're simply not true.

The truth is, you're victorious! The truth is that the battle was never yours to begin with! The truth is, there's hope for your future!

You don't have to stay the same. Whatever battles you're facing within yourself, be it your habits and old ways of thinking, God can change you. God WILL change you. You're valuable to God! When you

You're valuable to God!

talk to God, He's listening. Don't let the guilt of your mistakes stop you from praying and talking to God. No matter what you've done, He still wants to hear from you.

The enemy would love for you to stop speaking to God because He's the One who has the power to forgive you, set you free, and to help you live right. No matter what you've done, God can wipe your slate clean. Just go to Him, confess your sins, and feel the weight of disappointment lift off your shoulders.

When you take your shame to God, He'll take your shame and replace it with His love. Worrying about messing up doesn't keep you from messing up. Being full of God's love is what's going to keep you. It's His love that saves you, not your perfection.

Psalms 86:5 (NCV)

5. Lord, you are kind and forgiving and have great love for those who call to you.

THIS CAN HELP SOMEONE

DAY NINETEEN

Get Rid Of Distractions

Following God's voice is like following your GPS. Have you ever followed Waze or Google Maps and accidentally miss your turn? You may have been in the car talking to your friends or listening to the radio, and the next thing you know, you hear a voice say, "Make a legal U-turn when possible." You look up and find yourself going miles out of your way, on top of adding more time to your trip. Now, your 20-minute trip turns into a 40-minute trip. The same thing can happen when you're following God's *God is constantly speaking to you...* voice. God is constantly speaking to you, but are you listening to His directions?

Often times, you hear a word from God, and you begin to go in that direction, but somewhere along the way, you get sidetracked. You get caught up in meaningless conversations, maybe you're paying too much attention to the things around you, or maybe you tuned out God's voice and turned Him down, because you feel like you can take it from here.

When this happens, you find yourself going the wrong way. Distractions will have you missing your turn, wasting time, and even stopping at places you have no business being at. All this, because you stopped listening to God's voice, and got distracted.

Sometimes, it takes telling the noise around you to SHUT UP, so you can hear what your next turn is going to be! Turn the radio down, turn the talking down, and listen for your directions. You don't want to waste time going the wrong way. You don't want to waste time in places you shouldn't be. You don't want to waste time! BUT, if you do, God is still faithful. He'll recalculate your route and get you right back on track to the path of fulfilling your calling and purpose in life.

Psalms 32:8 (NCV)

8. *The LORD says, "I will make you wise and show you where to go."*

THIS CAN HELP SOMEONE

DAY TWENTY

God Is Bigger Than Your Problems

What are your biggest problems right now? Are they financial? Are you dealing with relationship problems? It could be with a friend, spouse, boyfriend, girlfriend, or maybe with your children. Do you have health problems? Are your co-workers your biggest problem? Maybe you said *yes* to all these problems and could even add more. If so, there's great news for you today.

God is BIGGER than your problems! Whatever your situation is, God is bigger! If you have money problems, God is bigger. If you're going through a bad breakup, God is bigger. Even if you're having trouble in school, God is bigger. Can't get your kids to act right? God is bigger! Are you getting this? God is bigger, God is bigger, GOD IS BIGGER!

Stop magnifying your problems and start magnifying the solution, which is God. God will never leave you. He is always there, listening to your prayers, and ready to comfort you and fill you up with His love, peace, and joy. Your problems aren't sent to break you. They come to build you—to build character, patience, and PERSERVERANCE! People's lives will be changed through your perseverance! God sees who you'll become and He knows what it'll take to get you there.

Your problems aren't bigger than God.

Your problems aren't bigger than God. The all-powerful God, Creator of the universe, can change your circumstances in an instant. If you pray and your problems don't go away, it's because God is up to something bigger than your problems. Sometimes, what He's doing goes beyond your thinking and beyond your understanding. You have to come to a place where you trust God when you understand, and you trust God when you don't. At the end of the day, you can find comfort in knowing that God will work everything out for your good.

When you come out on top, and YOU WILL COME OUT ON TOP, you'll look back on your problems and say with confidence, "Yes, my God is definitely BIGGER."

Psalms 46:1 (NCV)

1. God is our protection and our strength. He always helps in times of trouble.

THIS CAN HELP SOMEONE

DAY TWENTY-ONE

Honesty Is The
Best Policy

"You ain't got to lie Craig, you ain't got to lie." This popular quote taken from a 90's movie couldn't be any truer. Just replace "Craig" with your name and there you have it. There's not one person who can say they've never lied. Sometimes lying seems more convenient, like the better option, or like it's the only option, but those are just lies from the enemy. You really don't *have* to lie. It's a choice, every time.

Under what circumstances do you find yourself telling lies? Is it to get the better job, to impress a girl or guy, to get a better deal, or to get out of that ticket? You may think lying is harmless, and not a big deal, but it's actually a huge deal, and detrimental to your growth as a person.

When you lie, you're making a decision not to trust God. God wants you to depend on Him in every situation and circumstance, but lying says, "No God, I have to bend the rules here, because this is way over your head. There's no way you could possibly work this out for me, so I have to lie this time."

Is that what you believe? Do you believe that God can't get you the job without you lying on your resume? Do you think God can't send you your spouse without lying about who you are on a dating site? Do you think God can't soften your boss' heart, so you lie about why you were late to work? Do you think God can't fix your broken relationships, so you lie to cover up your wrong doings? Do you think God can't provide all of your needs, so you lie on your application for government assistance?

What areas in your life do you feel you have to lie, because you are not trusting God? Do you know that, what could take us a lifetime to accomplish, God can do it in a second? Don't minimize or downplay God's power. He can work things out for you in the most bazaar ways, leaving you standing in complete awe of His greatness.

God loves you and cares about everything you are going through. Whatever He allows to happen to you, know that it will work out for your benefit. God already knows your entire life and has already gone before you to handle all of your problems. Will you trust that God loves you and will provide solutions, without you having to lie?

God loves you and will provide solutions...

Honesty is the best policy, but more importantly, honesty is the godly policy.

Proverbs 12:22 (NIV)

22. The LORD detests lying lips, but he delights in people who are trustworthy.

THIS CAN HELP SOMEONE

DAY TWENTY-TWO

Stop Arguing

One of the greatest things we can do, here on Earth, is love people. The more you love, the more opportunities you'll have to impact your family, friends, and even strangers in a supernatural way.

Love draws people to God. Love causes people to say, "Hey, there's something different about you." And love brings peace during the trials and tribulations of life. Yes, love is absolutely amazing and rightfully so; considering God IS love.

So what can hinder you from love? ARGUMENTS. Sometimes, you can get so caught up in doctrine, religion, and judgment that you argue the love right out of yourself and out of other people.

Sooner or later, you're going to have to realize that God is God all by Himself! There is no one before Him and no one will come after Him. He IS...PERIOD! He is the ALPHA. He is the OMEGA. He is ALL POWERFUL. He is WISDOM. He is PERFECT. He is ETERNAL. He is ALL-KNOWING. He is FAITHFUL. He is the TRUTH. He is the CREATOR. He is SALVATION. He IS! Are you getting this?!

God calls us to LOVE people not LABEL them.

God doesn't need you to fight His battles! God calls us to LOVE people not LABEL them. If

94

someone doesn't understand your relationship with God or maybe has different opinions of the Bible, pray for them and pray for yourself as well, so that you may be a light.

Arguing with people is not your calling. Love is your calling. Stop trying to get your point across so that you can add a "W" to your spiritual belt. It's not about winning arguments.

Enough with making points! Instead, make it a point to LOVE.

2 Timothy 2:23-24 (NLT)

23. Again I say, don't get involved in foolish, ignorant arguments that only start fights. 24. A servant of the Lord must not quarrel but must be kind to everyone, be able to teach, and be patient with difficult people.

THIS CAN HELP SOMEONE

DAY TWENTY-THREE

Don't Be Scared

You don't have to be scared of the enemy! The enemy comes to steal, kill and destroy you, but guess what? You serve a God that came to bring life, AND bring life more abundantly! The Giver of life is on your side! You don't have to fear what the enemy's plans are for your life because God has the final say.

Everything that the enemy throws at you is filtered through God first. If God allows the enemy to mess with you, know that He has a plan far greater than what the enemy's plans are for you. As a matter of fact, if the enemy knew how God would work it all out for your good and make things EVEN BETTER for you, then the enemy wouldn't have messed with you in the first place! But he does, hoping that you will lose faith in God, hoping that you will quit, hoping that you will stop trusting God. Don't do it! Don't lose your faith! Don't Quit! Don't stop trusting! You will overcome!

God has not forgotten you and will never forget you. The enemy can't take what is God's. You

God has not forgotten you and will never forget you.

belong to God. The enemy tries to borrow you, borrow your life, but it's not his! The enemy is so weak. He's so weak! If you speak of God, the enemy will leave you alone.

Don't let the enemy shut you up. Keep talking! Talk of God's goodness, power, mercy, and grace. Talk about His awesomeness! TALK ABOUT IT! Watch the world around you change. Your atmosphere will change and the enemy will flee from you. You don't ever have to be scared of the enemy's attacks. They may seem strong, but God is stronger!

In the book of Exodus, God separated the sea so that His people could walk through the sea on dry ground without drowning. Yes, God moved water out of the way for His children! And do you know what happened next? Their enemies tried to come through the sea, so God CLOSED the sea on them! Yes, God CLOSED the sea! There wasn't any dry ground for their enemies to walk on!

So you see, you don't have to be scared because your enemies are somewhere drowning!

Exodus 14:28-29 (NCV)

28 The water returned, covering the chariots, chariot drivers, and all the king's army that had followed the Israelites into the sea. Not one of them survived.29 But the Israelites crossed the sea on dry land, with a wall of water on their right and on their left.

THIS CAN HELP SOMEONE

DAY TWENTY-FOUR

God has a plan for your life and He'll give you the tools to accomplish His plans. BUT...YOU STILL HAVE TO WORK. The dreams, goals, and aspirations God has put inside of you will require hard work, dedication, and perseverance. The work may seem overwhelming or maybe even frustrating at times, but you can rest assured that God will be with you every step of the way. You just have to take the steps.

You can't expect your dreams to come true while you sit back and watch reality shows all day. You can't expect your dreams to come true while you spend hours playing video games. You can't expect your dreams to come true while you spend all of your free time on social media. You can't expect your dreams to come true while partying all the time and sleeping too much. God has a great purpose for your life and you need to be awake to fulfill it!

God has a great purpose for your life...

Stop hitting the snooze button every morning! Laziness is not of God. He wants you to get up and work. Wake up early to work on the visions God has given you. Start moving towards your purpose. Start trusting that God will help you. Begin that leap of faith everyone raves about! It's truly an amazing way to live; moving, trusting, and leaping!

Believe that God will make provisions for you. Actually, believe that the provisions are already made! When you begin to pursue your dreams, God will step in and connect you with the right people and resources. The plans are already worked out for you! You just have to move forward and receive them. Even when you don't feel like moving, you have to move, knowing your help is on the way.

God doesn't leave you to work on your vision alone, because it's not yours! God gave you that passion. God gave you that dream. God gave you that vision. He's in this with you, trusting you to do everything He created you to do, and trusting you to be everything He created you to be. He's going to see you through all of the ups and downs, good times and bad times. He's with you! You don't have to work alone.

Sometimes, your work will be physical and sometimes, your work will be spiritual. There's going to be seasons of "foot-to pavement" where you're working nonstop and there's going to be seasons of "knees–to-floor" where you're praying and seeking God for your next move. Seek out God's strength, provision, and wisdom in both seasons. Don't get too busy working that you forget who your supervisor is.

God has so much in store for you. There are so many things set before you to accomplish that will change your life, and the lives of others, but it will require work. Make a decision today to work diligently at everything God has shown you to do.

John 4:34 (AMP)

34. Jesus said to them, My food (nourishment) is to do the will of Him Who sent Me and to accomplish and completely finish His work.

Stikks

Your Thoughts

THIS CAN HELP SOMEONE

DAY TWENTY-FIVE

What You Say Matters

God SPOKE the world into existence. You were created in God's image. There is POWER in your words! Just like God spoke and things happened, when you speak, THINGS HAPPEN. You have the ability to speak blessings over your life or curses over your life. This is HUGE!

You have the ability to speak blessings over your life...

Listen, if your life seems to be in shambles, feeling like you're carrying the weight of the world on your shoulders, then SAY SOMETHING! SPEAK UP! Speak against chaos, disaster, disease, low-self esteem, unemployment, laziness, poverty, depression, suicide, fear, anxiety, lust, greed, pride, loneliness, addictions, abuse, ANYTHING preventing you from enjoying the life God gave you. Speak against it! Speak and watch things change!

Declare your strength in the Lord! Speak peace over your life. Command worry and doubt to leave you at once. Tell stress and discouragement to flee immediately. Give defeat an eviction notice, because you are victorious. You are a winner, not a loser! THERE IS POWER IN YOUR WORDS! Your words affect your life and your words affect the lives of those around you.

The things that come out of your mouth will affect you and people in your atmosphere. Your friends, children, parents, co-workers, classmates, spouse, and neighbors will all be affected by the words you speak to them.

Take seriously how much weight your words hold and be cautious of what you say TO people and ABOUT people. Just a few words can kill someone's hopes, dreams, visions, and passion. A few words can destroy someone's life.

More often than not, when a child is bullied, it's verbal bullying, verbal attacks, and verbal abuse. It's not always physical. A child's self-esteem will be blackened before their eye is, and a lot of us are blackening our own self-esteem with negative self-talk.

Speak well of yourself to yourself! Speak well of yourself out loud. Speak well of others. SPEAK UP and SPEAK LIFE!

Proverbs 18:21 (MSG)

21. Words kill, words give life; they're either poison or fruit-you choose.

THIS CAN HELP SOMEONE

DAY TWENTY-SIX

Money Is Not Everything

Money is not everything…but being rich is! You've got to be rich in love, rich in peace, rich in joy, rich in wisdom, rich in patience, rich in humility, and rich in faith! These riches are priceless treasures that money will never be able to buy. These riches will add more value to your life than any check ever will, and these riches last!

Money, on the other hand, goes faster than it comes! No matter how much you make, you always seem to need more, it never seems to be enough, and there's always something new to buy. Money and stuff won't ever be the key to satisfaction or true contentment.

Your bank account doesn't reflect your value. Your bank account doesn't reflect your value. Your credit score doesn't reflect your value. The car you drive, the house you live in, and the clothes you wear, doesn't speak of who you are!

How much money can you take with you when you die? How much money do you need to have a successful marriage? How much money would it take to make your kids listen? How much does it cost to add additional days to your life? How much money do you need before you are completely content with what God has given you TODAY?

Some people want a financial blessing from God, while all the time, He's trying to bless you with riches most celebrities are still chasing after. Don't let television, music, and social media trick you into believing that life can only be enjoyed once you have money. That is a huge lie! Don't buy into it.

People have sacrificed their faith, family, and friends all in efforts to make more money. It's easy to get caught up in this world and forget about what really matters—like caring for the poor, widows, orphans, the sick, and inmates. Helping others and making an impact in people's lives is what matters.

Are you being a light in this world full of darkness and greed or are you focused on getting the spotlight on you? Are you generous with your time and finances, willing to serve others, so people can see the love of God in you? Are you available to your friends and family when they need you? Or are you too busy chasing money to have time for these things?

God will take care of you. God will provide for you. Stop chasing money and chase after the One who can truly make you rich.

Hebrews 13:5 (NLT)

5. *Don't love money; be satisfied with what you have. For God has said, "I will never fail you. I will never abandon you."*

THIS CAN HELP SOMEONE

DAY TWENTY-SEVEN

Cravings Are Not Your Boss

YOU decide what you eat. YOU decide how much you eat. And, YOU decide how often you eat. When it comes to your eating habits, some days may be better than others or your diet may completely suck. If this is the case, then it sounds like you're allowing your cravings to be the boss. YOUR CRAVINGS AREN'T THE BOSS. Stop being controlled by your cravings and start telling your cravings *No!*

Say *no* to that second helping. *NO,* to cakes, pies, and desserts every day! *No,* to the drive-thru window and *no,* to depending on caffeine every morning! What if you depended on the Word of God every morning like you depended on your cup of coffee? How different might your days look?

Today is the day that you FIRE YOUR BOSS. There's no need to put in a two weeks' notice. You can resign TODAY! Tell your cravings, "Enough is enough!" and take back your diet; TAKE BACK YOUR HEALTH! No more allowing your cravings to boss you around, telling you that you need sugar, caffeine, and junk all day. The only thing you need is some self-control.

Self-control is key when it comes to living a healthy lifestyle.

Self-control is key...

Self-control and discipline can change your life drastically, and self-control is actually a gift from God. If you feel like you're lacking in the area of self-control, pray! Pray and ask God to give you more self-control. When you get those cravings, pray, because God wants to help you!

Do you want to live a life that completely honors God? Are you honoring God in every area of your life, BUT your health? Maybe you're honoring God with your finances, talents, business, work, hobbies, wardrobe, speech, parenting and relationships, but when it comes to your diet...it's a free for all. You may be eating whatever you crave without considering how much sugar, calories, fat, and cholesterol you're putting into your body.

God gave you your body and anything that comes from God is a gift. Your life, your body, and your health are gifts from God. The Creator of heaven and Earth saw it fit to create you! How are you treating your precious gift?

God desires for us to seek Him and depend on Him for everything, including your health. Are you dependent on God when it comes to what you choose to eat and drink? Are you giving God a "say-so" in your diet or are you the god of your health? God is perfect in all of His ways. He created you; therefore, He knows exactly what you need to keep your body healthy. Submit your eating habits to God today. Exercise self-control and...EXERCISE your body. Your cravings aren't the boss, God is.

Romans 12:1 (NLT)

1. I plead with you to give your bodies to God because of all he has done for you. Let them be a living and holy sacrifice-the kind he will find acceptable. This is truly the way to worship him.

Stikks

Your Thoughts

THIS CAN HELP SOMEONE

DAY TWENTY-EIGHT

If Jesus had 12 disciples, why do some people think they don't need anyone? Needing people doesn't make you weak. Needing people doesn't make you inadequate, and needing people doesn't make you *needy*. You've heard it said before that "two are better than one," yet people tend to go through seasons of isolation, which often results in loneliness.

Do you know who wants you to feel isolated and alone? The enemy! The enemy loves to get you alone, away from your family and friends, to fill you with lies. When the enemy gets you alone, he'll use that as an opportunity to lie to you. The enemy will begin to tell you lies about yourself, lies about others, and lies about God. Before you know it, you'll be thinking you're worthless, nobody cares, and God isn't listening. These are all lies from the enemy, and it's easy to fall into the trap of believing these lies. DON'T DO IT! Don't believe them, not even for a second! You're a child of the KING! God cares DEEPLY for you and God listens to His children!

If you've been feeling alone and could use a few good friends around, pray for them. Pray that God will send you friends to strengthen, encourage, and support you. God will do it! Also, ask God to help you be the kind of friend you're looking for. Begin to be

...be intentional about building godly relationships...

intentional about building godly relationships and watch God begin to surround you with people who genuinely love and care about you! EVERYONE ISN'T FAKE.

You don't have to do or live life alone. God didn't design you to do life all by yourself. There are people you're supposed to learn from, and there are people who will learn from you. Don't isolate yourself. Say 'hello' to someone. Smile at people. You'll be surprised how far a hello and smile can go.

We all need people, and that's OK. Needing people doesn't make you needy; just human.

Ecclesiastes 4:10 (NCV)

10. If one falls down, the other can help him up. But it is bad for the person who is alone and falls, because no one is there to help.

THIS CAN HELP SOMEONE

DAY TWENTY-NINE

Use Your Gifts

When you buy someone a gift, typically you buy it in hopes that they will use whatever it is you've bought them. No one buys a gift hoping that it will never be used. In fact, a gift is typically given in hopes that it will be something of good use, and if it becomes someone's favorite thing, then you've hit the gift giver jackpot!

Everyone loves giving a good gift, knowing that it's being used over and over again. It makes you feel like the gift was appreciated and not a waste of money, time, and energy. How horrible would you feel spending hours, days, or even months looking for the perfect gift for someone, only to find out they never even opened it. You wouldn't feel too good about that, right?

So here's a question: How much more do you think God is expecting you to use the gifts He has given you?

You weren't born to sing, dance, act, draw, write, design, build, cook, teach, preach, (fill in whatever your gift is), for your own benefit. God put these gifts in you to change people's lives, and to benefit others. Whose life has been changed through your gifts?

There are people who can sing a wig off someone's head, yet you'll only overhear them singing in the shower or while they're washing dishes. THAT'S NOT RIGHT! Don't use God's gift on dishes! Your gifts are meant to bless people out there. God wants to reach people through you and your gifts.

It's not by random or chance that the gifts have come so naturally to you, while others have absolutely no way at being even mediocre at the things you're good at. People always talk about how they wished they could sing, or they wished they were taller, or faster for sports, because then they would use those gifts.

Stop looking at other people's gifts and start operating in your own God-given gifts. God has filled you with talents. God put something special in you. It may not look as extravagant as the person next to

God put something special in you.

you, and that's OK! God has specific assignments just for you that are just as important. Don't get so envious of other people's gifts that you neglect your own.

God doesn't give bad gifts! He's the ultimate gift giver! If there were a grab bag, you would want Him to pull your name! Be responsible with your gifts, and ask God what He wants you to do with them.

No one is responsible for your gift, but you. Fear is not an excuse to sit on your gifts pretending that you're not good at anything. You may be looking for God to elevate you in a particular area in your life, all the while, He's waiting for you to do what you were created to do. Use your gifts and watch God begin to use you.

1 Peter 4:10 (NCV)

10. Each of you has received a gift to use to serve others. Be good servants of God's various gifts of grace.

Stikks

Your Thoughts

THIS CAN HELP SOMEONE

DAY THIRTY

Don't Gamble On Your Eternity

This is your life..._____

THIS IS YOUR ETERNITY!!!!

_____

_____

_____

_____

_____

_____

_____

_____

_____

_____

_____

_____

_____

_____

_____

...And continue this for the rest of
FORRRREVERRRRRRRRRRRRR!

LIFE IS SHORT! That's not a cliché. It's a fact. You've probably gone to school with someone who's already passed away. There's likely someone you knew last year that didn't make it into this year. Not only is this life short; it's unpredictable. There's no guarantee that you will make it to be 70, 80, or 100 years old. So what are you living for?

Are you living for this world, which you'll pass through sooner than you know, or are you living for eternity, which lasts FOREVER? Are you bold enough to gamble with your eternity? The way you live today matters! How you live your life will determine how you live out the rest of FOREVER.

Don't take a gamble on eternity saying things like, "Oh, I'll figure it out later. Oh, I'm not sure what happens after you die. Oh I don't believe in Hell...etc." IS IT REALLY WORTH THE GAMBLE? Would you gamble on your life?

If someone gave you a gun with one bullet in it, but the rest were empty, would you spin it and shoot yourself in the head for one million dollars? There's a great chance that you wouldn't land on a bullet, but would you take that gamble and risk your life? Most likely, the answer is NO. So why gamble with your eternity, which is far GREATER than this life?

God loves you so much that He sent His Son, Jesus the Christ, to die on the cross for all of your sins. Not some, but ALL OF THEM. All the bad things that you've ever done, Jesus took the punishment for it, and He did it for YOU. He did it so that you can receive forgiveness. He did it so you wouldn't have to guess or play Russian roulette with your eternity. He did it so that you wouldn't have to be eternally separated from God. Jesus died for YOU.

> *God loves you so much and desires a relationship with you.*

God loves you so much and desires a relationship with you. It's not by accident that you're reading this today. It's not by accident.

Today, make the decision to put all of your hope, trust, and faith in Jesus. You don't have to gamble with your eternity any longer. Jesus already did the work and paved the way for you.

If you truly believe this, ask God to forgive you of all the things you've done wrong. Ask Him to forgive you and He will. No matter what you've done, God is faithful to forgive you. Welcome Jesus into your life and into your heart NOW—today is your DAY OF SALVATION.

Romans 10:9-10 (NLT)

[9.] *If you openly declare that Jesus is Lord and believe in your heart that God raised him from the dead, you will be saved. 10. For it is by believing in your heart that you are made right with God, and it is by openly declaring your faith that you are saved.*

STAY CONNECTED!

Take a selfie with your book and tag @stikksmodel

Instagram: @stikksmodel

Facebook: @stikksmodel

Website: www.christianmodels.org

#thiscanhelpsomeone

Photography by Jeff Smith

Made in the USA
Monee, IL
31 October 2020